Henrique Sabino de Oliveira

Outsourcing of Prisons

Henrique Sabino de Oliveira

Outsourcing of Prisons

An analysis of the constitutionality of Brazilian
Bill 2.825/2003

Imprint

Any brand names and product names mentioned in this book are subject to trademark, brand or patent protection and are trademarks or registered trademarks of their respective holders. The use of brand names, product names, common names, trade names, product descriptions etc. even without a particular marking in this work is in no way to be construed to mean that such names may be regarded as unrestricted in respect of trademark and brand protection legislation and could thus be used by anyone.

Cover image: www.ingimage.com

This book is a translation from the original published under ISBN 978-3-330-75596-3.

Publisher:
Sciencia Scripts
is a trademark of
Dodo Books Indian Ocean Ltd. and OmniScriptum S.R.L publishing group

120 High Road, East Finchley, London, N2 9ED, United Kingdom
Str. Armeneasca 28/1, office 1, Chisinau MD-2012, Republic of Moldova, Europe
Printed at: see last page
ISBN: 978-620-8-05660-5

SUMMARY

This study aims to trace the evolution of sentences worldwide, as well as the places where they are carried out, culminating in today's prisons. Bill 2.825/2003 will be studied, which aims to allow the outsourcing of activities ancillary to penal execution, as an alternative to improving the poor conditions in Brazilian prisons. Finally, obstacles will be pointed out that make this bill unconstitutional.

Keywords: Outsourcing; Prisons; Bill No. 2.825/2003.

SUMMARY

1) <u>Introduction</u>

The situation of the Brazilian prison system is in a calamitous state, proving to be completely ineffective, since it fails to fulfill one of the main purposes for which it was created: the re-socialization of the convict.

Despite the fact that Brazil has a Penal Enforcement Law (Law No. 7.210/84) capable, at least in theory, of solving prison problems, what exists in prisons is a contingent of people excluded from society, miserable people who are condemned to have their rights annulled, to enter a situation of anonymity and being stigmatized, without even having the prospect of a future, which their own present has been denying them.

Since it is not new news that the Brazilian prison system is in a state of decay, along with the huge shortage of places in existing establishments, it is extremely important to come up with new alternatives to solve this serious social problem. In this way, the inefficiency of the state in the management of prisons has aroused the interest of the private sector.

There are several proposals before the Brazilian government. They range from the outsourcing of middle-level activities to the total privatization of prisons.

Initially, this study will look at the evolution of sentences and penal executions on a global and Brazilian level, and then analyze the current conditions in national prisons.

Next, Bill No. 2.825/2003, presented by Federal Deputy Sandro Mabel, will be analyzed. It aims to amend the Penal Execution Law, so that the outsourcing of some activities ancillary to penal execution, at a national level, is allowed by the Public Power.

Finally, it should be noted that the intention of this work is to contribute to the academic and practical debate on the subject, and that it does not at any time intend to exhaust the discussion on the subject.

2) <u>Evolutionary aspects of sentencing and execution in the world</u>

2.1) The early days

Since the dawn of time, perhaps with the very emergence of life together, punishment has existed as man's response to the evil caused by one of his fellow human beings. As Ney Moura Teles sees it:

> [...] primitive man, as soon as he began to live in groups, felt the need to repress anyone who had harmed any of his members' interests and also to punish strangers who had set themselves against any individual or collective value (TELES, 2004, p. 18).

The member of the group was punished with the loss of peace, which consisted of his banishment from the tribe. The foreigner was punished with blood vengeance, including collective blood vengeance. In summary, Edilson Mougenot Bonfim and Fernando Capez teach that:

> When the offense was committed by a member of their own group, the punishment, as a rule, was banishment, known as the loss of peace, leaving the offender unprotected, at the mercy of rival tribes. If the offense was committed by someone outside the tribe, the punishment was revenge against the entire clan, including innocent people. It was a violent and almost always excessive revenge (BONFIM and CAPEZ, 2004, p. 43).

The penalties were strongly religious in nature, since peace came from the Gods and, once violated, vengeance was imposed as a form of punishment against the aggressor.According to Jose Henrique Pierangelli:

> [...] the origin of punishment is lost in the long night of time, coming from the most varied sources, but within a criterion of reasonable probability, criminal law would have its origin linked to religion, or religious superstition and punishment would have a sacred origin. (PIERANGELLI, 1995, p. 03).

Thus, in this period, penalties were characterized by a certain mysticism, stemming from the groups' connection to divinities. And, as a consequence of this religious link, the rules were given a divine character. Thus, if an individual violated a behavioral rule, the group rebelled against him, applying a sanction, with the aim of restoring the protection of the gods.

As mentioned above, punishments were characterized by private revenge, which was not subject to any criterion of proportionality. The evil of the crime was matched by another evil, in a form of blind reaction, unregulated by notions of justice.

During this period, the commission of a crime provoked a reaction not only from the victim, but also from their relatives and even from the entire tribe or clan. This led to the need to limit the scope of the penalty, so that it only affected the immediate and direct perpetrator of the crime.

It was in order to change this reality that, with social evolution, the thallion came into being, considered a great advance for the time, since it forbade retaliation against entire family groups and the destruction of the material goods that the aggressor possessed.With the thallion, proportionality was established between the conduct of the offender and the punishment, enshrining the discipline of giving life for life, an eye for an eye and a tooth for a tooth.

After this phase, the compositional system emerged, in which the victim or their relatives received a sum of money or goods, in the form pre-established by customary rules or rules written in legal texts, thus renouncing revenge and retaliation. In this way, the compositional system consisted of compensating for criminal offenses through a system of satisfaction or payment.

With better social organization, punishment, which was initially of private origin, was transferred to the public sphere, which, in the early days, maintained an absolute identity between divine and political power. At this stage, the objective of criminal repression was the security of the sovereign or monarch through penal sanction, which maintained the characteristics of cruelty and severity.

According to Luiz Regis Prado, the history of Criminal Law reflects the Social State and the ideas that characterize it, and the stages in the evolution of punitive justice can be divided as follows:

> [...] a) First epoch. *Crime* and offense against the gods. Penalty, means of appeasing divine wrath; b) Second epoch. *Crime* and violent aggression by one tribe against another. Penalty, blood revenge from tribe to tribe; c) Third epoch: *Crime* is transgression of the legal order established by the power of the State. Penalty is the reaction of the state against the will of the individual. Or they are presented as a *barbaric* conception, in which crimes are divided into public crimes, punishable by cruel corporal punishment, and private crimes, persecuted and repressed by the victim or his family; a *theocratic* conception, in which crime is always an attack on the religious order; and, finally, a *political* conception, in which crime is considered as a damage to the social order and punishment as a means of preventing and repairing it. (PRADO, 2001, p. 34).

2.2) Roman Criminal Law

According to Teles:

> [...] in Rome, since its formation, crime and punishment have predominantly had a public character, since crime was understood as an attack on the established order, and punishment was the state's response, although there were also primitive private punishments, carried out by the pater familias, who applied the thallion and the compounding. (TELES, 2004, p. 20).

Prado is more specific and describes with greater clarity and precision the way in which Rome differentiated between crimes and their penalties. In the author's words:

> [...] Roman law made a distinction between public and private offenses. The former, infringements of the social order, gave rise to public prosecution, while the latter were understood as offenses against the individual and authorized a private reaction, with the State interfering only to regulate their exercise (PRADO, 2001, p. 36).

The first written Roman code was the Law of the XII Tables, which began the period of legal diplomas, "imposing the necessary limitation on private vengeance, adopting the law of the thallion, as well as admitting composition" (BITENCOURT, 2008, p.30).The penal system of this Law was very advanced for the time. Most of the penalties described are types of pecuniary compensation for the damage caused.

2.3) German Criminal Law

German law was basically customary, since it lacked writing and dogmatic science, and was understood as an order of peace, whether public or private. A crime, in this sense, meant a breach, loss or denial of the established peace.

The reaction, in private cases, was carried out individually or through the family group, and the aggressor was handed over to the victim or his relatives so that they could exercise their right to revenge. In the case of offenses that were an offense to the whole community, the offender lost his peace, i.e. he was excluded from the family group and was at the mercy of everyone who had the right to kill him.

The Germanic peoples also knew and experienced blood revenge, "which only in later stages was gradually replaced by composition, voluntary, then compulsory" (PRADO *apud* BITENCOURT, 2008, p. 33).

As Prado rightly observes, German Criminal Law:

> [...] it was characterized by a peculiar and delineated system of compounding, which became the basis of its entire punitive system, which was distinguished

into three types: a) compounding paid to the offended party or his family group, by way of pecuniary reparation; b) the sum paid by the offender to the victim or his family, for the purchase of the right of vengeance; and c) payment to the tribal chief, the court, the sovereign or the State as a preacher of peace. (PRADO, 2001, p. 40).

2.4) Canonical Criminal Law

Canon Law is the law established by the Catholic Church, whose norms were written down in *canons,* which were equivalent to articles of law, in principle, regulating the internal life of the Church, imposing rules and disciplines on its members.

However, with the growth of the Catholic Church and, consequently, its influence on rulers, canon law began to be applied to other people, thus regulating the lives of the population in general, as long as the facts had a religious connotation.

Some of its characteristics, according to Teles:

> Firstly, he sought to establish a milder and more moderate system of punishment, with the abolition of the death penalty. His punishments were *spiritual* and *temporal,* the former consisting of penance and excommunication, all aimed at retribution for the evil done, but equally aimed at the defendant's repentance, and therefore called *medicinal* punishments (TELES, 2004, p. 24).

According to Cezar Roberto Bitencourt:

> Canon law contributed considerably to the emergence of the modern prison, especially with regard to the first ideas about reforming offenders. [It is said that the Church's ideas of fraternity, redemption and charity were transferred to punitive law, seeking to correct and rehabilitate the offender (BITENCOURT, 2008, p. 35).

2.5) Common Criminal Law

Common Criminal Law originated from local customs, mixed with elements of Feudal Law, Roman Law, Canon Law and Commercial Law.

Criminal legislation was characterized by cruelty in the execution of sentences, usually corporal and punitive, with the aim of social revenge and intimidation.

This right was applied without the possibility of the accused defending himself through a trial, and torture was the legitimate means of obtaining the truth.

In this context, Michel Foucault, in his work "Surveillance and Punishment", describes the trajectory of punishments, from the time when the deprivation of liberty, as a punishment, was linked to torture.

At that time, the punishment for evil was disproportionate, ferocious, savage and, above all, inhumane.

According to Armida Bergamini Miotto:

> [...] all the forms of penalty imposed, or made available for the judge to choose, had an accentuated function of "exemplarity", which can be broken down as follows: the "example" of punishment, suffering, humiliation, infamy, death of the condemned, should be intimidating; intimidation was, should be salutary against stimulation to crime. (MIOTTO, 1975, p. 27).

Suplicio, as explained by Foucault, was a corporal punishment, marked by dismemberment, amputation of limbs, marks on the face and exposure of the condemned person, dead or alive, to a spectacle in the form of a plague.

This type of punishment allowed the crime to be reproduced and turned against the criminal's body. It made their body the place where sovereign will was applied, the point where power was manifested.

In these public spectacles, the body of the condemned man was an essential part of the punishment ceremony. It was up to him to make his conviction and the truth of the crime he had committed known to everyone - because, up until this point, the criminal process had remained secret, taking place without the criminal's knowledge of the accusation, the charges, the testimony and the evidence produced.

However, the main character of this type of ceremony was the people themselves, whose presence was essential for it to take place. A supplication that was known, but which took place in secret, would be meaningless. The aim was to set an example not only by raising awareness that the slightest infraction risked serious punishment, but also by provoking an effect of terror through the spectacle of power over the guilty party.

The people not only had to know, but they also had to see with their own eyes. They had to be afraid, but they also had to be witnesses and guarantees of the punishment. Witnessing the ceremony was a right the people had; a hidden punishment was a privileged punishment, and it was often suspected that it had not been carried out in all its severity.

2.6) Humanitarian Period

To curb the excesses of common criminal law, the Enlightenment emerged, a humanitarian reaction resulting from the Enlightenment. At this time, ideas began to emerge that punishments should be moderate and proportionate to the crimes committed, given the completely inhuman nature of the punishment. This is because, according to Foucault, "in the worst of murderers, at least one thing must be respected when we punish: their 'humanity'" (1987, p. 95).

During this period, the Italian Cesare Beccaria, author of the book "Of Crimes and Punishments" (1764), vigorously combated the use of torture, the death penalty and the atrocity of punishments in general, pointing out that the penalty should only be applied so that the offender would not reoffend, as well as to serve as an example to the whole community. He called for the principle of legality to prevail, for clear criminal laws to be drawn up and defended a process in which the accused was guaranteed the right to a defense.

In this way, Beccaria's ideas ushered in what is known as the "humanitarian period" in criminal law and, after a while, some laws adhering to the precepts he advocated emerged.

Thus, the ideology of the body as the main target of penal repression began to disappear. At this point, the body was no longer the main object of punishment, but the soul. Punishment should act on the heart, intellect, will and disposition of the criminal. Noting that the right to punish shifted from the revenge of the sovereign to the defense of society, Foucault argues:

> In bodily supplication, terror was the support of the example: physical fear, collective dread, images that must be engraved in the memory of the spectators, like the mark on the face or shoulder of the condemned. The support of the example is now the link, the speech, the decipherable sign, the staging and display of public morality. It is no longer the terrifying restoration of sovereignty that will sustain the ceremony of punishment, but the reactivation of the Code, the collective reinforcement of the link between the idea of crime and the idea of punishment (FOUCAULT, 1987, p. 129).

From then on, punishment was seen differently: it was the sentence itself that marked the offender with a negative sign. In this context, debates and sentences began to receive a certain amount of publicity.

The theory of punishment on the soul represented the first move away from the excessive force of the sovereign towards more generalized and controlled means of punishment. However, the shift towards imprisonment that followed was the result of a new ideal focused on the body, which would have been developed in the 18th century: the technology of discipline and the ontology of "man as machine".

- The disciplinary method

According to Foucault, the establishment of prison as a generalized form of punishment for all types of crime was the result of the development of discipline in the 18th and 19th centuries. The author's analysis focuses on the creation of well-defined forms of discipline, targeting the most detailed aspects of each person's body. In his conception, modern institutions demanded that people and their bodies be individualized according to their purposes, and also for training, observation and control.

The historical moment of the disciplines - the second half of the 18th century - was the one in which an art of the human body was born, aimed not only at increasing its abilities, nor at deepening its subjection, but also at forming a relationship that, in the same mechanism, made it both more obedient and more useful. Discipline thus produced submissive and trained bodies - "docile" bodies.

Most of the time, the disciplinary process requires the existence of "fences", i.e. places that are heterogeneous to all others and closed in on themselves. Examples include religious colleges and military barracks.

For Michel Foucault:

> The disciplinary space tends to divide itself into as many parts as there are bodies or elements to divide. The effects of indecisive distribution, the uncontrolled disappearance of individuals, their diffuse circulation, their unusable and dangerous coagulation, must be annulled; this is a tactic of anti-displacement, anti-displacement and anti-agglomeration. It's important to establish presences and absences, to know where and how to find individuals, to establish useful communications, to interrupt others, to be able to monitor everyone's behavior at every moment, to evaluate it, to sanction it, to measure qualities or merits. A procedure, therefore, for knowing, mastering and using. Discipline organizes an analytical space (FOUCAULT, 1987, p. 169).

Discipline, in these terms, had to be imposed without excessive force, through careful observation, so that bodies were forged correctly. This led to the need for a particular form of institution which, according to Foucault, is well exemplified by Jeremy Bentham's Pan-opticon.

The Pan-opticon was the ultimate embodiment of a disciplinary institution. It consisted of constant observation characterized by the "unequal view". In fact, perhaps the most important feature of the Pan-opticon was its *design,* thanks to which the prisoner could never know when (and if) he was actually being observed. In this way, the "unequal view" determined the internalization of disciplinary individuality, and the docile body required by the inmates. This means that those in prison were less inclined to break laws or rules, since they believed they were being watched, even when, in reality, surveillance was not momentarily practiced. Therefore, the prison, especially if it wears the paradigm of the pan-opticon, offers the ideal form of modern punishment. According to Foucault, this is why the generalized, "gentle" punishment of chains and forced labor had to give way to the prison. The latter was the ideal modernization of punishment, and it was therefore natural that it would prevail over time.

- The rise of the prison

How could imprisonment not be the penalty par excellence in a society where freedom is a good that belongs to everyone in the same way and to which everyone is bound by a universal and constant feeling? The loss of freedom has the same nail for everyone: it is equal punishment. What's more, it makes it possible to quantify the penalty precisely according to the variable of time. By taking time away from the convict, prison seems to concretely translate the idea that the offense has harmed not only the victim, but society as a whole.

At its heart, the prison was like a small barracks, a school without indulgence, a gloomy workshop. In principle, it was intended for animals. They were not differentiated, however, between irrational and rational "inferiors". Men were bound by the feet, hands, neck, etc., according to fear or anger. Men and animals were tied up, chained, shackled, manacled, etc. The growing number of prisoners was a pretext for walling them up, packing them in and bolting them down. Caves, natural or not, underground, tombs, dungeons, pits, towers, everything was used to imprison them. They were imprisoned to prevent them from escaping or to force them to work.

However, from the 18th century onwards, the nature of imprisonment began to change, since it was adopted as a penalty in itself, and not just as a means of achieving punishment, since it was understood that this would eliminate the pointless torment and cruelty of other forms of punishment.

With this change, prison became the essence of punitive power, with the aim of isolating and rehabilitating the offender. It was understood that infected prisons, capable of making their inmates sick and killing them before their time, would be replaced by the idea of a public, severe, regulated, hygienic, impenetrable establishment, capable of preventing crime and re-socializing those who committed it.

It is important here to highlight the figure of the Englishman John Howard. It was Howard who inspired a penitentiary trend concerned with building appropriate establishments to carry out custodial sentences. According to Cezar Roberto Bitencourt:

> His ideas were extraordinarily important, considering the predominantly vindictive and retributive concept of punishment and its foundations in his time. [...] With a profound humanitarian sentiment, he never accepted the deplorable conditions in English prisons. [...] It is unquestionable that his ideas were very advanced for his time. He insisted on the need to build suitable establishments for the enforcement of custodial sentences, without ignoring the fact that prisons should provide prisoners with hygiene, food and medical care to cover their basic needs (BITENCOURT, 2008, p. 40-41).

In this context, the modern punitive system was built from the second half of the 18th century onwards, and two prison systems developed in the United States deserve to be highlighted.

One of these systems was that of Philadelphia, instituted in 1790, also known as the cellular system. In this system, convicts were confined to their cells 24 hours a day. It was in the cells that the convicts slept, ate and worked. This method was intended to stimulate remorse, repentance, meditation and prayer. The prisoners were kept away from the outside world and separated from each other, and the only reading allowed was the Bible.

In Foucault's words:

> [...] Isolation of the convict from the outside world, from everything that motivated the offense, the complicities that facilitated it. Isolation of inmates from each other. Not only must the sentence be individual, it must also be individualizing. And this in two ways. Firstly, the prison must be designed in such a way that it itself erases the harmful consequences that it attracts by bringing together very diverse convicts in the same place: stifling the plots and revolts that might form, preventing future complicity or the possibility of blackmail (on the day the inmates are free), creating an obstacle to the immorality of so many "mysterious associations". In short, that prison does not form a homogeneous and solidary population from the criminals it gathers (FOUCAULT, 1987, p. 265).

The other system was adopted in the 1820s in a penitentiary in the city of Auburn, in the state of New York, which imposed cellular isolation at night, but with work and meals in common. However, the silence was absolute and the surveillance permanent, meaning that the prisoners were forbidden to talk to each other or exchange glances, and could only address the guards after being authorized and in a low voice.

According to Luis Francisco Carvalho Filho, quoting Rotham:

> [...] At the heart of both systems was the idea that the criminal is the result of a failure in the process of building his character, a process normally promoted by

the family, church, school and community. The penitentiary would act precisely where those institutions had failed: in imposing routines, in encouraging reflection, work and repentance, in discipline and in handing out physical punishment to those who disobeyed the rules of confinement. (ROTHAM *apud* CARVALHO FILHO, 2002, p. 25).

And, according to the author:

[...] the advantage of the Auburn system over the Philadelphia system was the possibility of adapting the prisoner to an industrial routine: working in workshops for eight or ten hours a day offset the investment costs and gave the prison a more rational profile. (CARVALHO FILHO, 2002, p. 25)

Thus, the Auburn system ended up prevailing in the United States. The method of absolute isolation was immediately identified as a form of cruel punishment.

In fact, both systems proved impractical due to the growing number of prisoners and the high cost of building penitentiaries with individual cells. In addition, these systems offered no stimulus to inmates, as they were limited to obeying the behavioral routine and work imposed by the prison administration, as well as having to wait for time to pass.

It was on the basis of this reality that the progressive system of serving sentences was developed in Europe, which would later become the most appropriate to the ideals of regeneration.

In this progressive system, the prison sentence was served in three stages: an initial period of cellular isolation during the day and night, with hard labor and scant food; a period of common labor under the rule of silence, with isolation at night, in which the prisoner would acquire vouchers that could take him to the third stage; and finally, parole, where the prisoner would be relatively free for a fixed period, and if he didn't give cause to revoke the benefit, he would acquire definitive freedom.

Over time, the progressive model was perfected in Ireland, where a fourth stage was included among the established phases: the intermediate prison. In this phase, before being paroled, the prisoner worked outdoors, in special establishments, without the rigors of a closed prison.

Prison was therefore seen by society as the most effective way to combat crime in every sense. And today, it still has this conception. However, it is not only society outside the prison walls that needs to be satisfied, but also society that is incarcerated. Unfortunately, it is common knowledge that prison conditions in our country are shameful.

3) <u>Evolutionary aspects of penal sentences and executions in Brazil</u>

Before 1500, the primitive societies that existed in our territory were still at the stage of private revenge, with the presence of the talion and the loss of peace. It is true, however, that the Law of the primitive inhabitants of this land had no influence on the formation of Brazilian Criminal Law, so that, in order to talk about its history, we must first talk about Portuguese Criminal Law.

In this way, the historical evolution of Brazilian juridical-penal thought can be summarized in three main phases: the colonial, imperial and republican periods.

3.1) Colonial period

Colonial Brazil began in 1500 and ended around 1822. At the beginning, when Brazil was occupied by the Portuguese, the first legislation that came into force was called the Afonsinas Ordinances, the same as in Portugal, consisting of rules from Roman, Canon and Customary Law. It was still a time of public vengeance and, as such, some of its characteristics could not fail to be: the cruelty of the penalties, the non-existence of the right of defense and the principle of legality, arbitrary penalties and unequally fixed by the legislator.

According to Rene Ariel Dotti (1998), imprisonment at that time was generally preventive in nature, since it consisted of preventing the perpetrator from fleeing until his trial. In addition to its preventive function, imprisonment was also applied as a means of coercion to force the perpetrator to pay the financial penalty. However, in some rare cases, it appeared as a typical repressive reaction.

Fortunately, these rules had little or no application in our territory, as they were only in force until 1514, that is, in the first years after the Portuguese arrived in Brazil.

Thus, in 1514, the Ordenagoes Manuelinas were published and were definitively ready in 1521. According to Eduardo Bueno (2003, p.145), the purpose of this new law was to satisfy the vanity of King Manuel, and it was a copy of the previous code, plus some extravagant laws.

Criminal law was so cruel that imprisonment was not, as a rule, a criminal penalty, but rather a precautionary, procedural measure, since it was intended to guard the condemned until the execution of the sentence, which could be death, corporal punishment, affliction or torment. In addition, although rare, there was the penalty of servitude, which subjected the Moor or Jew who posed as a Christian to captivity.

The Manueline Ordinances were in force during the first century of the Brazilian colony's existence, and criminal law was applied by the grantees of the hereditary captaincies, who, as lords, judges and true kings, interpreted, said and executed the law as if they were gods.

In 1603, the Manueline Ordinances were repealed, and the Philippine Code came into force, famous for its severe punishments. This book totally ignored fundamental human values, containing a vast number of prohibited behaviors and numerous extremely brutal punishments.

According to Bueno (2003, p.144), the personal conditions of the defendant were of great importance in determining the degree of punishment, since individuals from lower social classes were reserved for the most severe punishments, while the nobility were guaranteed certain privileges. These distinctions were also relevant when it came to the sex of the defendant.

The legacy of this code is marked by the disproportion between the crime committed and the penalty. Edgard Magalhaes Noronha describes some types of penalty:

> The "morra por ello" was to be found at every turn. In fact, the death penalty had various forms. There was death simply by hanging (natural death); death preceded by torture (cruel natural death); death forever, in which the condemned man's body was suspended and, as it putrefied, it fell to the ground, remaining so until the bones were collected by the Brotherhood of Mercy, which happened once a year; death by fire, until the body was made into dust (NORONHA, 2001, p. 55).

In addition to corporal punishment, the infamous punishments cannot be forgotten, in which human beings were exposed in a vexatious way, with the aim of destroying their morals and good reputation. The principle of the personal nature of punishment, which is still in force today, was completely unknown, because the shame of the person who suffered humiliation was often borne by generations.

However, it is obvious that, even back then, some people were left out of this reality, such as noblemen, knights, squires and judges.

3.2) Imperial Period

The imperial period began in 1822, when Brazil gained its independence from Portugal. However, the Philippine Code was not repealed immediately, since a new code had to be drawn up first. Nevertheless, Prince Pedro, one month before September 7th, abolished torture and some cruel and infamous punishments, as well as determining the adoption of the principle of personal responsibility and prohibiting the transmission of punishment to the convict's successors.

In this new phase of Brazil, political, human and social values were restructured and the country developed under the mantle of social freedom. The European Enlightenment movement had a major influence on the creation of the fundamental principles of our Criminal Law (the principle of non-retroactivity, the personal nature of the penalty, etc.).

In this period, prison became not only an instrument of class protection, punishment and atonement, but, according to Dotti (1998, p. 50), "it also came to be seen as a source of amendment and moral reform for the convict".

In this way, the deprivation of liberty became an authentic and proper criminal sanction to replace corporal punishment, which had a broad spectrum in the ordinances.

In 1824, the first Brazilian Constitution was granted. It guaranteed public freedoms and individual rights. The new law foresaw the need for a criminal code, which should have pillars based on justice and equity.

In 1830, under the influence of the Classical School, the Criminal Code of the Empire came into being, incorporating the principles of moral responsibility and free will, according to which there is no criminal without evil, without knowledge of evil and without the intention of practicing it.

The penalties set out in the Criminal Code were: death by hanging, for the crimes of slave insurrection, aggravated homicide and robbery with death; gallows for forced labor, in which the condemned wore heels and iron chains; simple imprisonment and imprisonment with labor; banishment; banishment and banishment; fines and suspension of rights. These punishments were applied to free people, since slaves, who were considered to be semi-livestock, were still punished by the august punishment. Prison began to have a function of amendment and moral reform for the condemned.

As Dotti *apud* Carvalho Filho (2002, p.37) rightly points out, "this is an important change from the old regime, since the death penalty was envisaged for more than 70 (seventy) offenses".

For Carvalho Filho:

> [...] the main novelty of the Criminal Code of 1830 was, in fact, the emergence

Later, while the Empire was still in force, the death penalty was completely abolished due to a miscarriage of justice. Farmer Manoel da Mota Coqueiro was sentenced to hang for murder. However, some time later, errors were discovered in his trial.

The changes that followed the advent of the Criminal Code were enormous, so much so that they culminated in the abolition of slavery and the Proclamation of the Republic, events that occurred at a time when attempts were already being made to draw up a new Code.

3.3) Republican Period

In 1889, Brazil became a republic with the military coup of Marshal Deodoro da Fonseca. Faced with some social advances, such as the Aurea Law, the old Criminal Code of the Empire urgently needed to be replaced.

Decree No. 847, of October 11, 1890, converted the project into the Penal Code of the United States of Brazil. According to Schecaira and Correa Junior (2002, p.41), in the face of so many changes, the penalty still retained its instrumental character, both of prevention and of repression and social domination.

Given the circumstances in which the Code was created, jurists of the time criticized it for its technical imperfections and the deficiency of its concepts. In this sense:

> [...] it was drawn up hastily and before the Federal Constitution of 1891, without taking into account the notable doctrinal advances that were being made at the time as a result of the positivist movement, which is why it had serious technical defects and appeared to be behind the science of its time. (FRAGOSO *apud* PRADO, 2000, p. 67).

With the advent of the 1891 Constitution, new fundamental principles were incorporated, such as: "no one shall be sentenced except by the competent authority, by virtue of a previous law and in the manner regulated by it"; "no sentence shall pass from the person of the offender", and it expressly prohibited gallows sentences, banishment and the death penalty, except for military crimes in wartime.

Faced with a flood of laws and strong tendencies to revise the Penal Code of 1890, the government promoted a consolidation of existing laws, because "there were difficulties not only in applying extravagant laws but also in knowing them" (DOTTI, 1998, p. 58).

In 1934, the Constitution of the Republic was promulgated. The new charter abolished the penalties of banishment, death, confiscation of property and those of a perpetual nature, with the exception of declared war.

In 1937, with the arrival of the Estado Novo, changes in the political arena influenced criminal law. The Federal Constitution was granted by President Getulio Vargas, under the prism of authoritarian and military power. Congress was closed, political crimes were created and the death penalty reappeared. At this time, individual rights and guarantees were limited on the grounds of the public good and state security.

The new Minister of Justice, Francisco Campos, appointed Professor Alcantara Machado to study the changes to the penal law and make the necessary alterations. Alcantara Machado's preliminary draft provided for sentences of imprisonment, detention, segregation and fines. The draft also adopted the dual system (sentences and security measures), in addition to the effects of conviction, the publication of the sentence, confiscation and disqualification.

On December 31, 1940, the new Penal Code was published. Based on the Alcantara Machado Preliminary Draft, the Penal Code had Nelson Hungria as its main drafter.The National Congress was still closed.This Code is characterized, according to Shecaira and Correa Junior, by "legal technicality and disregard for criminology" (2002, p. 43).

In 1946, a new Federal Constitution was promulgated. It limited the punitive power of the state and "formally enshrined the individualization and personality of the penalty. In this context, Law 3.274/1957 declared the need to individualize the penalty" (SHECAIRA and CORREA JUNIOR, 2002, p. 44). The authors go on to say that "the purpose of criminal punishment was centered on special prevention, in other words, the social rehabilitation of the convict was sought" (2002, p. 45).

The military coup took place in 1964. However, the criminal laws were not changed immediately, as the formal guarantees of the legislation were of no use against the actions of the armed police, influenced by the military dictatorship.

The 1969 Penal Code was granted by the ministers of the Navy, the Army and Military Aeronautics, along with the New National Security Law. The death penalty, perpetual imprisonment and the 30-year prison sentence for political crimes were revived, and procedural guarantees were reduced.

The Constitution of the Republic of 1069 expressly provided for the purpose of special prevention in article 37, "proclaiming that penal execution should be promoted in such a way as to exert an individualized educational action on the convict with a view to his social recovery" (DOTTI, 1998, p. 79).

The 1969 Penal Code was known for the longest *vacatio legis* in our history, and was repealed by Law n. 6.578/78. Constitutional Amendment 11, of October 13, 1978, once again repressed capital punishment, perpetual imprisonment and banishment.

According to Ariel Rene Dotti:

> New paths opened up for the criminal sciences with the return of criminology and the greater attention paid to criminal policy. It was a return to theoretical discussions of crime and punishment as a social fact, with a view to the process of normative elaboration, which was becoming more democratic thanks to the political weakening of the government's "hard line" (DOTTI, 1998, p. 45).

3.4) The Penal Reform of 1984

Law 7.209, of July 11, 1984, reformed the general part of the 1940 Penal Code. This reform brought with it the abolition of accessory penalties (interdiction of rights, publication of the sentence, confiscation of certain assets and expulsion of foreigners). In the words of Sheicaira and Correa Junior:

> The publication of the sentence, due to its infamous nature, was abolished and the loss of public office became a necessary effect of the criminal conviction. Local exile was also abolished because of its infamous nature (SHECAIRA and CORREA JUNIOR, 2002, p. 46).

The double binary system was also abolished and our system is now governed by the vicarious system.

Based on this reality, in 1984 the general part, which deals with the basic principles of the Penal Code, was completely reformed, introducing new and modern concepts. A new system for serving sentences was consolidated, with the possibility of progression and regression of sentences and the possibility of new types of sentences (the so-called alternative sentences), including community service and the restriction of rights. In addition, in the same year, Law No. 7.210/84, known as the Penal Execution Law, was enacted, which comprehensively and positively reformulated the rules governing the enforcement of sentences.

Although the 1984 reform was brought about under the auspices of an authoritarian political regime, it was still a major step forward in the democratization of criminal law, as it enshrined the most modern principles of criminal due process.

3.5) Law 9.714/98

With the promulgation of the Federal Constitution of 1988, some updates were necessary, as the new Magna Carta brought new types of criminal sanctions and also innovated in the language used in the constitutional list of penalties.

This new law "inaugurated, in an untechnical and rather hasty manner, a new system of penalties in national legislation" (SHECAIRA and CORREA JUNIOR, 2002, p. 47).

Among the changes made by Stalei, the requirements for replacing the custodial sentence with a restrictive sentence are noteworthy. The jurist Miguel Reale Junior criticizes the abandonment of the prison sentence and the lack of strict criteria to guide the principles necessary for the substitution of the custodial sentence:

> Thus, a number of serious problems are generated by this legislation, which without a vision of the unity of the system and the interrelationship of the institutes, without an understanding of the proportionality that should illuminate the imposition of penalties, according to the value of the legal good affected, and expressed in the quantum of the penalty applied, has wiped out the harmonious and staggered whole that constituted the 1984 General Part. This is the result of the hasty thinking of the project's authors, whose vision prevented them from recognizing the whole and understanding the relationships between the institutes (REALE, 1999, p. 38-39).

4) **Brazilian Prison System**

4.1) Evolution of Prisons in Brazil

Quoting J. R. Russel-Wood, Luis Francisco Carvalho Filho states that:

> [...] in 1551 there was already mention of the existence in Salvador, Bahia, where the seat of the government-general of Brazil was installed, of a "very good and well-finished jail with an audience house and chamber on top [...] all made of stone and clay, plastered with lime, and roofed with tiles". (RUSSEL-WOOD *apud* CARVALHO FILHO, 2002, p. 36).

In 1551, the beginning of Brazilian colonization, prisons were located on the ground floor of town halls in cities and towns, and were a constituent part of local power. They served to collect rioters, runaway slaves and especially criminals awaiting trial and punishment. These prisons were not surrounded by walls, which allowed prisoners to maintain contact with passers-by through the bars. In addition, the prisons were also housed in fortified military buildings, which were built at strategic points for the defense of the territory. However, over time, these prisons lost their function.

Based on this reality, the Aljube, a former ecclesiastical prison in Rio de Janeiro, used for the punishment of religious, was given over by the Church to serve as a common prison after the arrival of the Royal Family in 1808.

However, in 1829, an inspection commission carried out in the Aljube stated that the environment in which the prisoners found themselves was terrifying, as there were 390 (three hundred and ninety) inmates, each of whom had an area of approximately 0.60 by 1.20 meters. By 1831, this number had risen to around 500 (five hundred) prisoners.

The Aljube was deactivated in 1856 and was defined, as Carvalho Filho (2002, p. 37) points out, as a "living protest against our living protest".

It was only with the decree of 1821 that the authorities became concerned about the state of the country's prisons. It was established that no one should be thrown into a narrow, dark or infected dungeon, because prisons should only be used to keep people and never to make them ill.

Three years later, with the advent of the Constitution of 1824, it was determined that prisons should be "safe, clean and well ventilated, with various houses for separating prisoners according to their circumstances and the nature of their crimes" (CAMPANHOLE *apud* CARVALHO FILHO, 2002, p. 37).

It was only with the Criminal Code of the Empire of 1830 that custodial sentences were introduced into our legal system. At that time, it was determined that the old means of punishment, such as the death penalty and hanging, would be reserved for cases of homicide, murder and slave insurrection.

Based on this reality, two establishments were designed, one in Rio de Janeiro and the other in Sao Paulo. These were the Houses of Correction, inaugurated in 1850 and 1852 respectively, which symbolized the country's entry into the era of punitive modernity. The Houses of Correction had workshops, courtyards and individual cells. They sought to regenerate convicts through regulations inspired by the Aurburn system, according to which prisoners worked in silence during the day and went back to their cells at night.

As Carvalho Filho rightly observes:

> [...] the two Houses of Correction, islands of excellence, a kind of rupture in the existing punitive reality, did not fail to mirror the general situation of a slave-owning and repressive country, since in addition to housing prisoners sentenced to imprisonment with labor, simple imprisonment and also the gallows, they housed correctional prisoners, not sentenced, made up of vagrants, beggars, troublemakers, Indians and minors arbitrarily locked up by the authorities. (CARVALHO FILHO, 2002, p. 39).

The Houses of Correction also had a special enclosure, the so-called calabougo, designed to house runaway slaves or slaves who had been handed over by their owners to the public authority as a deposit, so that they could receive the sentence of aggravation.

As Fernando Salla rightly points out:

> [...] throughout the Empire, a culture on the subject began to form in the country, with jurists and officials traveling abroad to learn about prison systems. The creation of maritime, agricultural and industrial penal colonies was debated. Concern was raised about the scientific study of the personality of the offender. The criminal came to be seen as a patient, the penalty as a remedy and the prison as a hospital (SALLA, 1999, p. 134).

At this time, the feeling that the country was not treating its prisoners properly was consolidated. Because of these conditions, the format of the Houses of Correction was the object of various criticisms, since there was the impression that the regime adopted, instead of regenerating and moralizing the delinquent, tended to corrupt him even more.

In 1890, with the advent of the Republican Code, the ideal system for the purposes of a modern nation became the progressive one, in which the force and the gallows disappeared from the punitive scene. In addition, temporary sentences restricting individual freedom were introduced, which could not exceed 30 (thirty) years, a rule that prevails to this day.

Under the Republican Code, the basis of the sentencing system was cellular imprisonment, provided for the vast majority of criminal conduct, which had to be served in a special establishment, where the prisoner would have a period of isolation in the cell and then move on to compulsory work in common, with nighttime segregation and daytime silence.

According to Dotti:

> [...] the 1890 Code created other measures to deprive individuals of their liberty, but they were more restricted in their application: imprisonment, for political crimes, in fortresses, war plagues or military prisons; disciplinary imprisonment, for vagrant minors up to the age of 21 (twenty-one), in industrial establishments; and imprisonment with labor, for vagrants and capoeiras, dancers of the rasteira and berimbau, in agricultural penitentiaries. (DOTTI, 1998, p. 55).

In 1920, the Sao Paulo penitentiary was inaugurated in the Carandiru neighborhood. It was a milestone in the evolution of prisons and was visited and considered by jurists and scholars from Brazil and around the world to be a model regenerative institution.

The penitentiary, built for 1,200 prisoners, offered the most modern prison facilities: workshops, infirmaries, schools, technical staff, adequate accommodation and security.

As Salla observes:

> [...] the new penitentiary was part of a broad project of social organization drawn up by the elites of the period, in which a prison should match the material and moral progress of the state (SALLA, 1999, p. 185).

However, it had the vices and violence of any other prison, where disciplinary rigor is exercised according to subjective criteria.

Quoting Salla, Carvalho Filho states that:

> [...] Furthermore, the very disciplinary structure of the time, based on the rule of silence among prisoners, did not prevail in practice, since according to reports, the "dead" in prisons communicated by "conventional signals" and by "pipes from the sanitary appliances that communicate with neighboring cells." (SALLA *apud* CARVALHO FILHO, 2002, p. 42).

It wasn't until 1940 that the Penal Code was published, which has remained in force to this day. The new system created two custodial sentences: imprisonment for more serious crimes, with a maximum sentence of 30 (thirty) years, which subjected the convict to daytime isolation for up to three months and then common labor within the penitentiary or outside it, in public works, and detention for sentences of a maximum of three years, where inmates had to be separated from prisoners and could choose their own work, as long as it was educational.

However, as Fragoso notes, quoted by Carvalho Filho:

> The separation order was not obeyed by the Brazilian authorities, and the practical differences between imprisonment and detention disappeared over time, with only the procedural ones remaining valid (FRAGOSO *apud* CARVALHO FILHO, 2002, p. 43).

Prison was considered the backbone of the new system created in 1940, as around 300 (three hundred) offenses defined in the Penal Code were punishable by deprivation of liberty (imprisonment or detention).

Then, with the advent of the Criminal Offenses Law, in 1941, 69 (sixty-nine) minor offenses were defined, providing for 50 (fifty) of them the penalty of simple imprisonment, to be served without penitentiary rigor.

Another building, symbolic of the history of Brazilian prisons, was the São Paulo House of Detention, also located in Carandiru, which housed more than 8,000 men, when its capacity was only 3,250 (three thousand two hundred and fifty) prisoners.

The Casa de Detengao was inaugurated in 1956 for prisoners awaiting trial, but its purpose became corrupted over the years, as it began to house final convicts as well. It became known worldwide for the squalor of its interior and for its extensive record of riots, escapes and episodes of abuse and violence, especially the massacre of 111 (one hundred and eleven) prisoners in 1992 by the Military Police.

The House of Detention was decommissioned in 2002, and the initiative was dubbed "the end of hell", where more than 7,000 prisoners were promised to be transferred to 11 new, smaller and more distant prisons.

In 1977, with the partial reform of the Penal Code, the view began to prevail that prison should be reserved for more serious crimes and dangerous offenders. However, it wasn't until the 1984 reform that the movement became more pronounced, since, among other measures, alternative sentences were created.

4.2) Purpose of the Prison Sentence

When we talk about prisons, there are three main purposes: retributive, preventive and resocializing.

The first is that provided for by law (the amount of penalty awarded for the harm caused individually or collectively).

The preventive purpose is characterized by the example that the punishment given to an individual generates in the rest of the community. However, it is worth noting that the example of punishment can be reversed - impunity goes in the opposite direction to prevention.

Perhaps the main purpose of the prison sentence is resocialization. It will do no good for an individual to leave the prison walls the same way they entered. In this sense, the Penal Execution Law preaches work and education as the main pillars for achieving this goal. With these two tools, the prisoner has a chance of being reintegrated into society.

According to Augusto Thompson:

> The purpose of the prison sentence is officially proposed as the achievement of not one, but several concomitant objectives, such as: retributive punishment for the harm caused by the offender; prevention of the commission of new offenses by intimidating the convict and potentially criminal people; and regenerating the prisoner, in the sense of transforming him from a criminal into a non-criminal (THOMPSON, 2002, p. 03).

As stated above, of these three fundamental objectives of the custodial sentence, the resocializing purpose stands out, since the Penal Execution Law in its article 1 states that: *"The purpose of penal execution is to carry out the provisions of a criminal sentence or decision and to provide conditions for the harmonious social integration of convicts and internees."*

In addition, other provisions can be found in the Penal Execution Law that aim to re-socialize the convict, such as the various forms of assistance, including the progression of regimes, assistance to former convicts, all with the aim of reintegrating the convict.

Nevertheless, Thompson points out that:

> Despite the energy used by the legal precepts, which converge in the sense of highlighting, in particular, rehabilitation as one of the aims of prison sentences, the purposes of punishment and intimidation remain untouched, and there is no rule authorizing them to be disregarded, to a greater or lesser extent, if necessary, for the benefit of reeducational activity. In other words, if there is operational friction between the various purposes, the relaxation of those purposes in favor of the latter has no legal support. Or again: Officially, the goal of recovery takes precedence, but it is not allowed to be achieved at the cost of sacrificing the goals of punishment and intimidation (THOMPSON,

2002, p. 04).

However, in order to achieve the goal of re-socializing the individual, he must remain in a prison that is suitable for his rehabilitation. However, prison overcrowding, the inhumane living conditions of prisoners, the growth of criminal organizations and corruption within prisons, together with the lack of security, mean that prisons cannot fulfil their function.

4.3) Prison Reality

The poor conditions of incarceration characterize almost all of Brazil's prisons, and make us realize that our

he prison system is practically bankrupt. What "should be" (a place for resocialization, recovery), "isn't".

In this context, Superinteressante magazine, in its issue number 250, states that prisons "form a nation apart. A country with its own economy, driven by extortion, bribery and illegal trade. A place full of unwritten laws, imposed by organized crime" (SOUZA and VERSIGNASSI, 2008, p. 54).

According to the aforementioned magazine report, prisons are characterized by a unique system of their own, including "internal legislation", since the individuals in them have their own rules and sanctions. There is commercial competition for places among inmates, as well as the sale of drugs, food and drinks in general. In addition, prisoners set up their own clandestine telephone exchanges in order to speed up their communications with the outside world. Other than that, say Fatima Souza and Alexandre Versignassi:

> [...] Overcrowded, the prison system has turned into chaos. In 2002, there were 240,000 prisoners for 182,000 places, that is, 58,000 more prisoners than the prison system could handle. By 2007, this deficit had risen to 157,000 prisoners - 437,000 for 262,000 places (SOUZA and VERSIGNASSI, 2008, p. 56).

According to a report on the BBC Brasil website[1] , in May 2012, Brazil was submitted to the Universal Periodic Review - a monitoring instrument of the UN High Commissioner for Human Rights - with the recommendation to "improve prison conditions

---

[1] Available at: http://www.bbc.co.uk/portuguese/noticias/2012/05/120529_presos_onu_lk.shtml. Accessed on 26/02/2013.

and tackle the problem of overcrowding".

According to the non-governmental organization, the International Center for Prison Studies (ICPS), Brazil, with a prison population of around 500,000, is second in number of prisoners only to the United States (2.2 million), China (1.6 million) and Russia (740,000).

According to the most recent data from DEPEN (National Penitentiary Department), from 2010, Brazil has a number of prisoners 66% higher than its capacity to house them (a deficit of 198 thousand).

On the reality of prisons, Luiz Flavio Gomes points out in his article "Dignity and the prison system. Real functions of the prison sentence. State of Law 'versus' State of Exception" :[2]

> What we teach at university, what we write in books, what some authorities mention in their speeches and reports, what some judges say in their sentences, what is contemplated in the laws, what is preached by the Rule of Law has nothing to do with reality (which is purely a State of Exception). You have to throw off the mask. After hours and hours of study, classes, seminars, congresses, etc., a law student only has to visit a prison to see that everything he has learned about prison sentences *(law in books)* has nothing to do with the world of concrete experiences lived inside them *(law in action)*. There is a world of lies being told about prisons every day. This whole picture of barbarism can only be changed one day when all the masks come off (GOMES, 2012).

The 1998 Federal Constitution is based, among many others, on the principles of human dignity, freedom and equality for all citizens. However, the reality of Brazilian prisons is in conflict with these precepts, given the lack of structure in penitentiaries and prisons.

In the words of Elaine Maria Geraldo dos Santos, in her article "Saude

Mental Health and Human Rights in the Brazilian Penitentiary System" :[3]

> Contemporary Brazilian penal legislation remains far removed from prison reality: overcrowded cells, a lack of vocational training, the slow pace of proceedings in the Judiciary and violence inside prisons are some of the problems that contribute to aggravating the crisis in the country's prison system (SANTOS, 2005, p. 04).

And, according to Romualdo Flavio Dropa, in his article "Human Rights in the Brazil: Exclusion of Prisoners" :[4]

---

[2] Available at: http://static.atualidadesdodireito.com.br/lfg/files/2012/05/Dignidade-e-sistema-prisional.pdf. Accessed on 25/02/2013.
[3] Available at: http://www.revista.ufpe.br/revistatempohistorico/index.php/revista/article/viewFile/9/7. Accessed on 08/03/2013.

According to Dotti:

The prison crisis is an old penal and penitentiary problem, with a strong criminological character. It is basically determined by the structure of human and material shortages and has caused a new type of mass victimization in recent years, since rebellions have ceased to be a localized problem, inside the walls, and have taken on the proportions of community terror when the victims of kidnappings imposed as a condition for constitutional and legal guarantees multiply. There is a new legion of hostages manufactured by anomie and hopelessness. In addition to prison guards, mass victimization involves other perpetrators: the managers and technicians of prisons and the relatives of prisoners. Even children, taken by the calloused hands of women for their weekly visit, are part of this chain of new victims of institutional and private violence (DOTTI, 1998, p. 62).

Although Brazil has a Penal Enforcement Law capable, at least in theory, of solving prison problems, what exists in prisons is a group of socially segregated people who have no expectations of future improvement.

The inefficiency of the state in the management of prisons has thus aroused the interest of the private sector, which is presenting proposals to privatize and outsource this sector.

---

[4] Available at: advogado.adv.br/artigos/2003/romualdoflaviodropa/direitoshumanosdetentos.htm. Accessed on 08/03/2013.

5) **Bill No. 2.825/2003**

There are several proposals before the Brazilian government. They range from the outsourcing of middle activities, in which the administration of prisons would remain the responsibility of the state (mixed management), to the total privatization of prisons, importing foreign models.

In this context, we will now analyze Bill number 2.825/2003, which was authored by Federal Deputy Sandro Mabel[5] .

5.1) Difference: Outsourcing and Privatization

Initially, it is important to outline the main points that distinguish the concepts of outsourcing and privatization.

Outsourcing consists of partially delegating certain services to private companies, since the government has a monopoly on criminal enforcement. The private sector would be responsible for accessory activities, or middle activities.

Thus, the material management would be delegated to private companies and the operational management would remain with the state, constituting a mixed management.

In the words of Jose dos Santos Carvalho filho:

> It is entirely legitimate for the state to delegate some of its middle activities to third parties, contracting directly with the company to which the employees belong. This is the case with maintenance, cleaning and surveillance services. This is a case of licit outsourcing. However, it is forbidden to delegate end-activities, as is the case with institutional and proper functions of public bodies (CARVALHO FILHO, 2009, p. 179).

In outsourcing, the state will act in conjunction with the private party, as it will not delegate the *jus puniendi* to the latter, since it is an end-activity, but will allow the private party to provide services related to middle-activities. As a result, there are those who argue that the state will be able to more successfully achieve the purpose of the penalty, which is not just to impose a punishment, but to offer prisoners the opportunity to re-socialize.

[5]   Deputy Sandro Mabel. PMDB - GO. Member of the following Committees: Labor, Administration and Public Service, Consolidation of Brazilian Legislation, PEC 405/09 - Retirement for Garimpeiro, CPI - Slave Labor. Alternate member of the following Committees: Constitution, Justice and Citizenship, PL 6025/05 - Civil Procedure Code, PEC 010/11 - Executive Branch Goals Plan.

Privatization, from a restricted point of view, is conceptualized by Maria Sylvia

Zanella Di Piettro as the procedure that *"covers only the transfer of assets or shares of state-owned companies to the private sector"* (2003, p. 19).

More broadly, Cristiane Derani states that:

> [...] Privatization is the name given to the transfer of a service carried out by the public authorities to the private sector and also to the transfer of ownership of public production goods to private economic agents. In the first case, ownership of the service remains with the public authority, but its exercise is transferred to the private agent (...). Another way of transferring public power to the private sector, in addition to the power to carry out a certain activity, is the transfer of public ownership of production assets to the private sector. The state sells its assets, withdrawing from the productive activity it was carrying out - an activity that could be market or non-market. When selling its production assets, the state can sell companies that carry out activities in the collective interest, and which act directly in the market, but it can also sell production assets of those services that are its normative attribution and are developed outside of market relations (in this specific case, the sale of the asset will be linked to compliance with the conditions for the concession of the service). The property is sold to the concessionaire: the property follows the one who is considered in the bidding process to be capable of carrying out the public service (DERANI, 2002, p. 110).

At first glance, the term "privatization of prisons" may give the idea of transferring state power to private enterprise, which would use the labor of the incarcerated for profit. But what is actually intended is the transfer of prison administration to the private sector, without this implying the withdrawal of the state's function, which is non-delegable.

The management of prisons would be the responsibility of the private sector, with the government providing support through tax incentives and subsidies, as well as supervision and control, with the support of society and competent bodies such as the Public Prosecutor's Office.

5.2) Targeted changes

The purpose of this bill is to amend the Penal Execution Law, regulating the outsourcing of services within prisons.

The Deputy proposes that medical, legal, psychological, social, food and clothing, cleaning and security services can be provided by private companies. The bill also provides for the possibility of private hospitals providing in-patient or out-patient treatment for people who are criminally incapable, unimputable or semi-imputable, as well as for people with infectious diseases, drug addiction or the HIV virus.

According to Sandro Mabel, in his explanatory statement in the body of Bill 2.825/2003:

<blockquote>
With the outsourcing of services, there will in fact be a mixed management of prisons and juvenile detention centers, because, according to the proposal, the state will continue to have the power to appoint the respective managers, and the private sector will only be responsible for the operation of the aforementioned activities. It is not a question of unduly delegating any state activity, because the aspects relating to the enforcement of sentences will continue to be the responsibility of the state, particularly the Criminal Enforcement Judges.
</blockquote>

5.3) Arguments in favor of approving Bill 2.825/2003

If the bill is approved, it is argued that the state will be relieved of its burden, and will use the resources - then earmarked for these services - to invest in other sectors of society, or even to improve the physical structure of prisons.

According to information and reports on Sandro Mabel's own website[6] , the legal change is necessary because today's prisons do not promote the social rescue of inmates, but on the contrary, they worsen the situation of the people in this situation, further aggravating the issue of fighting crime and violence.

Faced with the alarming situation in which prisons find themselves, Joao Lopes argues[7] :

<blockquote>
Faced with this scenario, it is appropriate to advocate outsourcing prison services as a way of tackling the system's undeniable crisis. We are aware that the change cannot be implemented simply or with modest patches. But the need for change is a peaceful one and this timid study is only intended to show the paths that can be followed in the legal field or even at the administrative level of innovative experiments already underway in the country. This requires political will and the awareness that spending on the prison network is not only a humanitarian commitment to the dignity of prisoners, but also a strategic investment in crime prevention (LOPES, 2011).
</blockquote>

Taking a more analytical stance, Julio Fabbrini Mirabete agrees with outsourcing:

<blockquote>
Administrative-judicial activities can only be carried out by public officials or bodies, as provided for by law. Sentencing activities can be carried out by public bodies or by private individuals or entities, including companies. Penal establishments can be private or public buildings, managed and operated by private individuals or entities for the material execution of custodial sentences, as provided for by state law. This management and operation by a private company does not exclude the judicial activity of the execution judge and the administrative-judicial activities of the magistrate and the other execution bodies. The only activity that cannot be carried out by private individuals in penal establishments is the application of disciplinary sanctions, which, because it directly influences the development of penal execution
</blockquote>

---

[6] Available at: http://www.sandromabel.com.br/web/noticia/sandro-mabel-defende-terceirizacao- dos-presidios. Accessed on 04/03/2013.
[7] Available at: http://jus.com.br/revista/texto/18368/privatizacao-penitenciaria-legalidade-e- conveniencia. Accessed on 25/02/2013.

<blockquote>
(administrative-judicial activity), is assigned to a public body, in accordance with local law. (MIRABETE, 1992, p. 16).
</blockquote>

Luiz Flavio Borges D'urso is also in favor of this type of procedure:

<blockquote>
We are not transferring the State's jurisdictional function to the private entrepreneur, who will exclusively take care of the material function of executing the sentence, in other words, the private administrator will be responsible for the food, the cleaning, the clothes, the so-called hospitality, in short, the services that are indispensable in a prison. [...] the jurisdictional function, which cannot be delegated, remains in the hands of the State, which, through its judicial body, will determine when a man can be imprisoned, how long he will stay, when and how the punishment will take place and when the man can leave prison. (D'URSO, 1999, p. 44-46).
</blockquote>

5.4) Arguments against the approval of Bill 2.825/2003

There are positions against this type of operation, given that it is the exclusive responsibility of the state to maintain public order through the use of force, and the idea of delegating the services inherent in criminal enforcement to private individuals is completely absurd.

Carlos Eduardo Ribeiro Lemos criticizes this type of operation, claiming that profit will always speak louder for private companies, regardless of the real prison situation. Let's see:

<blockquote>
The idea of profit is what has raised the most criticism of corporate intervention in prison administration on moral and ethical grounds. We are not discussing the higher or lower cost of this type of activity, nor the efficiency of the services provided in relation to the dignified treatment of the incarcerated, but above all, the legality and convenience of outsourcing an activity that should be conceived as an essential function of the state, one of its raisons d'être: the administration of security and justice (LEMOS, 2007, p. 86).
</blockquote>

Recently, on January 28, 2013, the first prison complex to be built through a public-private partnership in the country was inaugurated in the city of Ribeirao das Neves (metropolitan region of Belo Horizonte).

During its construction, the complex already faced criticism for delegating prison services to a private entity. Firstly, it should be noted that, according to studies, the cost of this model is more expensive - the State Government of Minas Gerais will pay the companies responsible for the site R$2,700.00 (two thousand seven hundred reais) per prisoner, whereas the amount spent in the public system is around R$2,100.00 (two thousand one hundred reais) per prisoner[8] .

In this regard, it is worth mentioning Paraná's experience on the subject.

According to the Penitentiary Department of Paraná - DEPEN, the first outsourced prison built in Brazil was the Industrial Penitentiary of Guarapuava, in the state of Paraná. Inaugurated in 1999, the penitentiary was built with funds from the federal and state governments and was designed to house male prisoners in a closed regime. After the inauguration of PIG, the Parana state government built five more prisons and outsourced them to third parties: the Curitiba House of Custody, the Londrina House of Custody, the Piraquara State Prison, the Foz do Iguagu State Prison and the Cascavel Industrial Penitentiary. In fact, the state of Paraná took back full management of these prisons on August 2, 2006, and did not renew the contracts with the private sector, since these prisons cost twice as much as the public ones.

In addition to the cost, it is important to mention the arguments of the lawyer and advisor to the Pastoral Carceraria, Jose de Jesus Filho, in an interview given to the ClippingMP Portal[9] :

> [8]Available at: http://www1.folha.uol.com.br/cotidiano/1221899-mg-inaugura-primeira-penitenciaria- feito-com-parceria-privada.shtml. Accessed on 06/03/2013.
> [9] Available at: http://clippingmp.planejamento.gov.br/cadastros/noticias/2013/1/16/minas-abre- presidio-public-private. Accessed on 06/03/2013.
> I've visited many states that have tried. Some have given up, others have maintained the cogeneration system to this day. What I can say is that I saw a lot of things wrong. Prisoners tied up in their cells, with a nine-second time limit for showering, soap that had to last a long time. In short, private enterprise wants to make a profit. But the prison system can't provide that, it doesn't follow the logic of the business world.

According to Jose de Jesus Filho, the model of joint management of prison units lacks publicity and seriousness. He also claims that there were constant conflicts between the directors of the units, government representatives and the managers of the private sector. The Pastoral Carceraria advisor concludes:

> As the saying goes, you can't kill the donkey to get rid of the ticks. In other words, it's not because the prison system is doing badly that the state should hand it over to private enterprise. The right thing to do would be to tackle the real problem in the prison sector, something that has never been done. Prison means deprivation of liberty, and deprivation of liberty should not be delegated to third parties, it should be the monopoly of the state. While the public interest wants to ensure that people don't escape and, at the same time, that they are re-socialized, private initiative wants to maximize profits and reduce costs. This mix between public and private in the prison system is very delicate. What we have seen, in visits to establishments that use outsourcing, is a mishmash of data, a lot of propaganda and little practical effect. It is an illusion to think that the private sector is going to solve the problem of the Brazilian prison system. The motivation of the private sector is to make money. To do this, it's worth putting ill-prepared people to work, instituting strict rules, practicing torture, without the services being provided in return.

There are still some specific obstacles to this type of operation being fully realized.

- Ethical and legal obstacles

From an ethical and moral point of view, the delegation of public services relating to prisons to the private sector is reprehensible. Prison is, above all, synonymous with repression, one of the characteristics of punishment. It is therefore inconceivable that a company could commercially exploit a prison system based on making a profit at the expense of human repression.

The only morally valid coercion is that exercised by the state through the imposition and execution of penalties or other sanctions. Therefore, from an ethical point of view, it is inadmissible for anyone to enrich themselves with the punishment imposed on them.

On this subject, there is an important study by the American Eric Lotke. According to the author, the advantage of investing in prisons would be the lower costs of carrying out services in such establishments:

> [...] the great attraction of private prison management and service companies is simple: they can carry out the same work done by the government in prisons at a lower cost, usually 5% to 15% below public sector costs (LOTKE, 1997, p. 28).

According to Lotke, this would be possible at the expense of employee salaries and in the absence of investment in services that *"could transform prisoners into productive members of society upon their release"*, since *"profit-conscious companies prefer to avoid the costs of addiction treatment, group counseling, literacy programs"* (LOTKE, 1997, p. 28).

The greatest contradiction of the idea then arises: how can it be accepted that profits can be extracted from suffering itself? How can monetary gain be conceived from crime? Is this not a contradiction in terms?

Such a procedure is, above all, inhumane, something more to stigmatize the personality of the convict, transforming him, as said above, into an object of profit, and not of recovery (it is clear that it would not be in the interest of a private company to resocialize anyone, quite the contrary; a resocialized man would be one less in their cells).

There are those who say that the outsourcing under study is not prohibited by the Federal Constitution, and that, because of this factor, it would be permitted.

However, this analysis cannot be done in isolation, simply by looking for some constitutional provision that prohibits this procedure.

The Constitution must be read broadly and its interpretation, in this context, must be guided by all the principles present in the Brazilian legal system.

So how can we conceive of private enterprise making a profit from the suffering of those whose freedoms have been taken away? As mentioned above, many experiences have shown that terrifying practices are used to maximize corporate profits. Where is the respect for the dignity of the human person of prisoners? Are such practices constitutional?

- Political obstacles

In political terms, the involvement of the private sector in the penitentiary sphere has raised doubts as to the compatibility between the public nature of the decision-making process, inherent in the formulation of criminal policy, and the profit motive of companies.

An analysis based on a modest syllogism is enough to reach the conclusion that the model of private prison management is politically inappropriate: the theoretical objective of prison management is to fight crime and not to make a profit; now, the companies that wish to participate in prison management aim to make a profit and derive that profit from the very existence of crime; therefore, these companies that have an interest in maintaining their profits will not fight crime; and if they don't have such an interest, they shouldn't manage prisons.

In addition, outsourcing services inherent to prison activity to private entities would mean assuming the failure of the Brazilian system and also demonstrating the failure of the government to effectively rehabilitate inmates. Thus, to transfer prison activities to private individuals would be to deny the efficiency of public power itself.

6) <u>Conclusion</u>

The theoretical objective of a penitentiary is to fight crime, not to make a profit. Crime is not just a state problem, but a social one. Making it possible for society as a whole to participate in the rehabilitation of prisoners, so that they can return to society with a good guarantee that they will not return to crime, is the aim of the system.

If our prisons don't have the minimum conditions to house human beings (and this is true), it's up to the state, with the money it collects from taxpayers, to change the model we see today and ensure what little dignity is left to someone who has already lost their freedom. It's up to the government to find solutions that allow the sentence to be carried out in a humane and effectively re-socializing way, a process that also involves the professional preparation of the respective staff and an increase in the number of prisons, thus relieving the pressure on those that exist today.

In this sense, what must exist is humanization in the application of penalties, transforming it in such a way that it is possible for it to achieve its purpose of re-socializing the prisoner.

Seeking solutions in private proposals is not the effective solution to the problems facing the system. The solution to the Brazilian prison system lies in the laws themselves, which are not respected and applied, and in community participation in the process of executing the sentence, humanizing society's view of the prisoner and ensuring their reintegration into society.

What is really important in order to change the scenario of Brazilian prisons is to demand that the state and its representatives have the political will to change the prison model and structure that exists today, with immediate policies for improvement rather than outsourcing.

ADOLFO, Lucio. Criminal execution in Brazil. **Consulex Legal Magazine**. Brasilia: Consulxe, 2003.

ARAUJO JUNIOR, Joao Marcello de. **Privatization of prisons**. Sao Paulo: Revista dos Tribunais, 1995.

BECCARIA, Cesare. Of Crimes and Penalties. 2ª edition. Sao Paulo: Martin Claret, 2008.

BITENCOURT, Cezar Roberto. **Treatise on criminal law**, volume 1: general part. 13th edition. Sao Paulo: Saraiva, 2008.

BONFIM, Edilson Mougenot; CAPEZ, Fernando. **Criminal Law**: General Part. Sao Paulo: Saraiva, 2004.

BUENO, Eduardo. **Brazil: a History** - the Incredible Saga of a Country. Sao Paulo: Atica, 2003.

CARVALHO FILHO, Jose dos Santos. **Manual of Administrative Law**. 22nd edition. Rio de Janeiro: Lumen Juris, 2009.

CARVALHO FILHO, Luis Francisco. **Prison**. Sao Paulo: Publifolha, 2002.

CORDEIRO, Grecianny Carvalho. The Brazilian model of privatization of the prison system. **Revista Juridica Consulex**. Brasilia: Consulex, 2004.

DERANI, Cristiane. **Privatization and Public Services**: The Actions of the State in Economic Production. ia edigao. Sao Paulo: Max Limonad, 2002.

DI PIETRO, Maria Sylvia Zanella. **Partnerships in Public Administration**: concessions, permits, franchises, outsourcing and other forms. 4th edition, Sao Paulo: Atlas, 2003.

DOTTI, Rene Ariel. **Bases and alternatives for the sentencing system**. 2nd edition. Sao Paulo: Revista dos Tribunais, 1998.

DOTTI, Rene Ariel. **Criminal Law Course**: General Part. 2nd edition. Rio de Janeiro: Forense, 2005.

D'URSO, Luiz Flavio Borges. Privatization of Prisons. **Consulex Legal Magazine**. Brasilia: Consulex, 1999.

FOUCAULT, Michel. **Surveillance and punishment**: the birth of the prison; translated by

Raquel Ramalhete. Petropolis: Vozes, 1987.

LOTKE, Eric. The Prison Industry. **Brazilian Journal of Criminal Sciences**. Sao Paulo, Revista dos Tribunais, 1997.

MINHOTO, Laurindo Dias. **Privatization of prisons and crime**. Sao Paulo: Max Limonad, 2000.

MIOTTO, Armida Bergamini. **Course in prison law**. Sao Paulo: Saraiva, 1975.

MIRABETE, Julio Fabbrini. **The privatization of penal establishments in the face of Law No. 7.210, of July 11, 1984 (Penal Execution Law)**. Sao Paulo: Justitia, 1992.

PIERANGELLI, Jose Henrique. **Fasciculos de cidncias penais** - penas e prisões. Porto Alegre: Sergio Antonio Fabris Editor, 1992.

PRADO, Luis Regis. **Course in Brazilian criminal law**: general part. 2nd edition. Sao Paulo: Revista dos Tribunais, 2001.

SHECARIA, Sergio Salomao. **Criminal Studies in Honor of Evandro Lins e Silva**. Sao Paulo: Editora Metodo, 2001.

TELES, Ney Moura. **Criminal law**: general part. Sao Paulo: Atlas, 2004.

THOMPSON, Augusto. **The prison question**. 5th edition. Rio de Janeiro: Forense, 2002.

ANNEX

Bill No. 2.825, of 2003

(by Sandro Mabel)

Adds articles 77-A and 86-A to Law No. 7.210, of July 11, 1984, which "Institutes the Penal Execution Law", and makes other provisions.

The National Congress decrees:

Art. 1. Law No. 7.210, of July 11, 1984, shall come into force with the following amendments:

Art. 77-A. Activities relating to the assistance referred to in items I to V of art. 11 of this law, as well as security in penal establishments, including those for the internment of minors, may be carried out by contracted private companies, provided that the following requirements are met, in addition to others established in specific legislation:

I - prior hearing of the Penitentiary Councils, the Public Prosecutor's Office, the Brazilian Bar Association and the curatorship of minors;

II - selection of companies by means of a bidding process, the public notice of which shall require the bidder to provide proof of specialization in prison administration and custody of minors or, exclusively with regard to the latter activity, in hospitality, as well as specialized training of the professionals to be allocated to the services which are the object of the contract;

Sole paragraph. The directors of penal establishments, including those for the internment of juvenile offenders, shall continue to be appointed by act of the competent authority even in the event of outsourcing of the activities referred to in this article.

Art. 86-A. An administrative contract with the competent public body, preceded by a bidding process, may be signed by private institutions, or promoted by them, as long as authorized by the execution judge:

I - the internment or outpatient treatment of the criminally incapable or the unimputable and semi-imputable, referred to in arts. 99 and 101 of this law, including in relation to the treatment of chemical or psychological dependency;

II - the serving of sentences by people with infectious diseases, drug addicts or carriers of the Acquired Immunodeficiency Syndrome virus;

III - the education of minors in custody, covering elementary and high school subjects, as well as guidance on social interaction and leisure;

IV - the integration of prisoners and inmates into society after they have served their sentence or completed their period of internment. Paragraph one. The construction and operating conditions of the hospitals referred to in the *caput* shall comply with the rules established by the National Criminal and Penitentiary Policy Council, as well as the norms contained in the specific legislation.

Art. 90. The penitentiary will be built in a place far from urban centers.

§ Paragraph 1 - Prisons located in rural areas must have an area set aside for the agricultural activities of convicts, from which part of the food to be consumed in the prison will be taken.

Art. 2. At least every one (1) year, the judge of penal executions shall receive a detailed report on the activities carried out by private institutions entrusted with the detention of prisoners and the internment of minors, detailing, among other information, the behavior displayed by prisoners and interns.

Art. 3 This law shall enter into force on the date of its publication.